J. B. Crocker

A Complete and Comprehensive Treatise on the Art of

Crayon Portraiture

In Black and White

J. B. Crocker

A Complete and Comprehensive Treatise on the Art of Crayon Portraiture
In Black and White

ISBN/EAN: 9783337340353

Printed in Europe, USA, Canada, Australia, Japan

Cover: Foto ©Thomas Meinert / pixelio.de

More available books at **www.hansebooks.com**

A COMPLETE

AND

COMPREHENSIVE TREATISE

ON THE ART OF

CRAYON PORTRAITURE,

IN

BLACK AND WHITE.

BY J. B. CROCKER,
Teacher of Crayon and India Ink.

PRICE, $1.50.

CHICAGO, ILL.:
THE JEWELERS' JOURNAL, 57 WASHINGTON ST.
1884.

CONTENTS.

INTRODUCTION.

RAWING was formerly looked upon as an accomplishment, or as a means of gratification by which time might be pleasantly occupied, or the tastes and talents of the artist displayed. But it has become one of the essential and indispensable features in the education of the present generation. The pleasures and advantages of its pursuits were formerly enjoyed by the rich alone, and its beauties and mysteries never revealed except to the favored few.

But in the present age Schools of Design and Academies of Fine Arts have been opened in all our large cities, and even our common schools are giving special attention to this branch of study, until it is almost within the reach of everyone to acquire some knowledge and skill in this direction. It cultivates habits of tastes, the appreciation of the beautiful in art, as well as in all the varied and graceful forms in nature itself.

Beside being classed among the accomplishments, it has already become one of the most profitable of employments. Thousands to day are engaged upon the periodicals, illustrated papers, art magazines, books, &c., which flood our land ; exhibiting not only their skill in this direction, but contributing to others, beautiful views of natural scenery in this and other lands ; the faces of public and prominent men : beautiful forms and designs for home decoration, for the brush, the pencil or the needle.

In fact every branch of trade and industry desire and find it necessary to illustrate the wares they offer for sale, so that drawing is indispensable to the practitioners of almost every art, trade, or profession.

Many hand-books have been published from time to time, treating of almost every branch or department in the Fine Arts, but as yet no book of any practical value has ever appeared describing the method of Crayon Portraiture in black and white.

The writer of this volume having been engaged for many years in teaching this beautiful art, at the earnest solicitations of his pupils has consented to publish this treatise, hoping it will prove valuable and useful to all who desire, or who would find pleasure in producing upon canvas the human face in its ever varying forms, features, and expressions.

He has endeavored to give careful and comprehensive instruction, pointing out the errors pupils are liable to make at the start, giving the simplest details, many of which will prove most useful to the student ; explaining the entire method so thoroughly that any one of average intelligence can, after a little practice, learn to execute a Crayon Portrait of real merit.

That such a book will find a welcome the author feels assured, and has no hesitancy in saying there are thousands who will hail it with delight, and gain from it just the knowledge they require to enable them to achieve excellence in this most beautiful and fascinating accomplishment.

CRAYON PORTRAITURE.

TO one who knows nothing of the art of Crayon Portraiture it seems not only very difficult, but almost unattainable. In fact, many suppose some natural gift is necessary to be able to produce the human features in life-like form upon the canvas. Such, however, is not the case. The writer has given instruction to hundreds of pupils, many of whom are now practicing this art as a profession, and instructing others. Any one who can learn to write can learn to draw, but yet it is necessary to have a special method in order to work intelligently. The author purposes to give a series of written instructions, which, if carefully followed, will prove invaluable, to all who desire to achieve success.

MATERIALS.

ONE of the first and most important factors toward success is to have the proper materials, and of the very best quality. Unlike most other branches of Art, the materials for Crayon work are few in number and inexpensive:

A Drawing Board, about 22x27.

An Easel.

A Rest Stick.

A piece of Chamois.

One soft rolled Chamois Stomp.

One dozen small Paper Stomps.

One stick of Square Contè Crayon, No. 3.

One stick of Round Contè Crayon.

One stick of German Crayon, No. 2.

One piece of Contè Rubber.

One Crayon Holder, (brass.)

A few sticks of Soft Charcoal.

One dozen Thumb Tacks.

A Block of Wood, 3x5, covered with fine Sand Paper.

A small Palette, covered with Chamois.

A Stretcher of Whatman's Paper.

A sheet of Manilla Wrapping Paper.

If it is desirable to save all unnecessary expense, many of these materials can be of home manufacture. An inexpensive easel will answer the purpose quite well, and a small slender cane will answer as a rest stick. The drawing board can be obtained at any Art Store, or a carpenter be employed to make one at a small outlay. The block of wood covered with fine sand paper, and the palette of paste-board covered with Chamois are easily made.

The former will be found useful in cleaning and sharpening the rubber and paper stomps. Another block may also be made and covered with fine emory paper, to be used in making a fine point to the German and Conté Crayons for point work. The palette is intended to be used for the pulverized Crayon, or Crayon Sauce, as it is often called, and when not in use should be carefully covered to keep it free from dust. The small paper stomps are sometimes called paperettes, and come in packages of a dozen or more. They will be found very useful, and a much more pleasing effect can be obtained than with the Chamois stomp, especially upon the face. Avoid the hard paper stomps made of pulp: they are worthless.

THE PAPER.

HERE are many varieties of paper that can be employed for Crayon Portraiture. Among these the most used, are Whatmans' Imperial and Double Elephant, Eggshell, Steinbach, and the French tinted papers; and many fine effects are produced upon them all. Almost every Artist has a choice, therefore no rule can be laid down to be followed implicitly.

The Whatmans' is however generally considered the most desirable. Do not however attempt to use even this by tacking it to a drawing board, but have it mounted on a stretcher. The hard surface of the drawing board would make irregularities in the work. These stretchers already prepared can be obtained at the Art stores, where Artists' Materials are sold. It is, however, presumed that many who read these pages may reside so far from such supplies, that it may seem desirable to understand how to make them

TO MAKE A STRETCHER.

PROCURE a pine frame 20x24, or any other size desired. Lay a sheet of Whatmans' paper upon the
drawing board, with the face side down, which can
be distinguished by the water mark in the paper, by holding it up to the light. Dampen it with a sponge or wet
towel, going over the entire surface of the paper; place
the pine frame upon it, and trim the edges of the paper
with a sharp knife about one inch larger than the frame.
Cut out the corners also. With a small brush put a little
flour paste upon the paper beyond the frame, and also
upon the edges of the frame.

Next with the fingers turn up the paper upon the edges
of the frame as smoothly as possible, drawing out the larger
wrinkles. Having turned all the edges up, take up the
frame carefully, and gently draw each of the four sides
one after the other, from the centre toward the corners,
and note that it adhers firmly. It is not necessary to draw
it so tightly that it looks perfectly smooth, as if drawn too
tightly it would split; the smaller wrinkles will all disap-

pear when it is thoroughly dry. Put this away in a cool room, not by the fire, and in a few hours it will be ready for use.

Care should be taken not to rub the paper on the side upon which the drawing is to be made. Avoid also putting the fingers on the face of the paper, as this would occasion spots, causing injury to the work.

CRAYON SAUCE.

C RAYON Sauce, or Pulverized Crayon, is made in the following manner: Take a stick of the No. 3 square crayon, and rub it on a piece of sand paper, or a file, holding it over the palette, and allowing the fine crayon thus made to fall upon the chamois palette. Make quite a little quantity of this upon different parts of the palette. Avoid having any little pieces of the crayon chip off, or if they do, grind them up by placing the crayon stick upon them and crushing them. Make this sauce as fine as possible. Next take a paper stomp and mix or grind the sauce until the palette is thoroughly saturated, and it is ready for use.

THE PHOTOGRAPH,

O R subject to be copied, should be the next consideration. It seems necessary to give a little advice upon this selection :

Do not attempt to copy a wood cut, they are often faulty in drawing, are almost always flat: the copy would be very unsatisfactory, and possibly discourage you from further attempts.

Neither attempt for a first picture to copy a tin-type, or a very small *card de visite*. It would be more difficult to get a correct enlargement, and the shadows would not be plainly defined.

A photograph from an ideal head would be the best selection one could make for the first attempt. First, because they are copies from a good crayon drawing, and present the grain effect that is so desirable; second, the result would be pleasing even if the exact likeness had not been attained.

This, however is optional with the student, but by all means, if the subject selected is to be a family portrait, select a good cabinet size photograph, one strongly defined, and properly lighted, and the result will be satisfactory.

THE ENLARGEMENT.

MANY artists use Solar Prints, and the working them up has been carried to considerable perfection. Certainly they can be finished with more rapidity, as they save much labor in sketching the outline, and it is much easier to obtain a correct likeness. The artist has merely to give the crayon tint, strength and roundness, with a little point work in the way of finish, and the portrait is complete. But such crayons are becoming more and more unpopular, since the public have learned what the process is, and an artist who works over solar prints exclusively, does not take rank with those who make a pure crayon portrait. They will always fade more or less when exposed for some time to the light, or turn a reddish tint and after a few years are worthless, but a pure crayon never changes.

The author is aware the above advice will meet with opposition from all copying houses, and such as persist in working over solar prints, but the facts are the same, and should be fairly stated. To such as may prefer to work them, the method described in this volume will be applicable.

There are several ways of making the enlargement. A solar print may be obtained and used for tracing, by blacking the back, and tracing with a stylus, as described later on.

Another method is by procuring a negative from the photograph, a magic lantern used, throwing the picture upon the stretcher the desired size, and tracing the outline in the dark, with a piece of charcoal, after which it can be finished up by the photograph.

In either or all cases, draw the outline upon a piece of manilla wrapping paper, in order to make all necessary corrections or alterations before transferring it upon the stretcher.

There is a system of squaring off a picture for enlargement, which was much used by the old masters, and is used to a great extent among the artists of to-day. It consists in dividing the picture to be copied into squares of equal size, and drawing squares upon the canvas or paper as much larger as the desired drawing is to be larger than the picture to be copied. Then, whatever is seen in each square in the smaller picture, is to be drawn in the corresponding square upon the paper for the enlargement.

For Portrait Artists the system in its simple form is not altogether practical, for the accuracy required in their

2

work, would necessitate the use of a large number of small squares, making the work too laborious and confusing to justify its very extensive use.

Other objections might also be brought to notice, but an instrument overcoming all objections to this method of enlargement, has been devised, and termed the Metroscope.

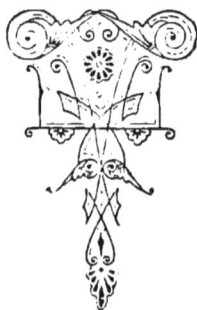

THE METROSCOPE.

HE meaning of this term is a measured view. It comprises several series of squares engraved upon the finest plate glass by machinery, thereby being perfectly accurate and durable. The two plates of glass, (of which one form of the instrument consists), are ruled for convenience with squares differing in size. These are framed and held together by thumb screws, allowing sufficient space between them for inserting and securing a picture of the size of a cabinet photograph, which bring the lines into perfect contact with all parts of the picture, giving the appearance of the lines being actually drawn upon the picture. One feature of this instrument which renders the square system the most practical for general use, consists of the division and sub-division of the squares by finer dash and dotted lines. The eye more naturally divides a line or space into halves and quarters, than any other proportions, and for this reason the dash lines have been designed for quartering the main squares, and the dotted lines for quartering the squares thus formed. This gives sixteen times as many squares for use as are drawn upon the paper, or are seen upon the glass at a little distance, and therefore will not cause any annoyance when the main or quarter squares only are desired to be used.

The benefit derived from this combination is the perfect ability of the draughtsman, with a little practice, to begin immediately to put in the values or principal shades of the picture, without having to make the entire outline of the drawing. A mere outline in the first place belongs only to drawing in proportion, and not in projection, as the shadows determine the latter. At a glance the form, size, depth and location of shadows are seen in relation to the squares of the instrument. Their location upon the paper is determined by the main squares drawn upon it, and other properties by means of the small squares. Where the greatest accuracy and most detail is required, lines forming the smallest squares may be drawn in at such places as are deemed necessary.

As many photographs stretch in the process of mounting in one direction more than the other, causing faces to appear either too long or too wide, this distortion should be corrected in the enlargement. When it is ascertained in what direction, and to what degree a picture is stretched, the squares may be made longer in an opposite direction upon the paper, to correct this distortion.

An ordinary cylindrical lens may be used in determining in what direction and to what degree a face is distorted.

The L or Differential Square has been devised to be used for squaring off the paper. It is of great assistance in rapidity and accuracy, and may also be adjusted to extend or contract the squares sufficiently to correct whatever distortion may exist in a photograph.

THE PANTOGRAPH.

HIS machine for enlarging or reducing pictures and drawings was said to have been invented in 1603, but it has since undergone many modifications and improvements. It consists of four metallic or wooden bars or rules, each rule being perforated with a series of holes by which they can be connected together by means of thumb screws. It is provided with a tracing and a marking point, and a screw or point which is forced into the drawing board to hold the instrument in position.

They are usually numbered from 1 to 20, on the four bars indicating sizes. There are a great variety of these instruments for sale, and many of the cheaper ones are worthless, the holes not being placed in the right position. The cheap instruments which sell for twenty cents may be classed among the number. For about $2.00 a good pantograph can be purchased at the Art Stores, and with proper care it will last a lifetime, and always be at hand whenever an outline is desired.

The thumb screws when placed in the number in one bar should always correspond with the number on the opposite one, otherwise a distorted outline would be the result.

In enlarging from a very small picture as a card photograph, the higher numbers will be required, say 15, 17, or even 18. But Cabinet or Imperial photographs can usually be enlarged to life-size by using the numbers of 12 or 14.

To use the instrument, select the number desired, secure it to the drawing board at the left hand side, place a piece of manilla wrapping paper at the other end of the board and secure it with thumb tacks. Next place the marking point in the centre of the paper, after which place the photograph under the indicating point in the centre also, and secure it to the board. This indicating point should always touch the photograph, and if it does not, place a little weight on the instrument, a silver half dollar, or if this is not sufficient add a few smaller coins, until this point just touches the photograph.

Now guide the instrument by taking hold of the marking point, but watch the tracing point. In this manner go over the entire photograph, putting in as many of the details as may seem necessary, indicating the position of the shadows, the folds in the drapery, the masses in the hair, and all other features, until a perfect enlargement is the result.

This can now be transferred to the stretcher as follows :

THE TRANSFER.

WHEN the outline is finished and all corrections made, rub the back of the paper over with a piece of charcoal, covering it thoroughly; shake it slightly that the fine particles may fall off, then place it carefully on the stretcher.   Measure the distance from the side of the head and shoulders on each side, as well as the top and bottom, and when the drawing is in the centre of the stretcher, or in the proper position, secure the four corners to the stretcher, by means of thumb tacks, or little weights, that it may not slip while tracing it.   Next take a stylus or a hard and sharp lead pencil, and bearing on gently, trace over all these outlines again, following them very accurately, and omitting none.   Remove the thumb tacks, lift the paper off gently, and a perfect outline of the original will be found upon the stretcher.   This outline being simply charcoal, will rub off with the slightest touch, and thus be destroyed; therefore place the stretcher upon the easel, and with one of the small paper stomps slightly blackened in the crayon sauce, go over all these outlines once more very lightly, in order not to lose them while at work upon the portrait.   Do not make these lines hard, or they will show when the picture is finished, and thus spoil the effect of the work.

LIGHT.

TO work to the best advantage proper light is necessary. A north light is considered the most desirable. Place the easel in such a position by the window as to allow the light to fall upon the stretcher from the left side.   There is one advantage however in crayon work over oil or water colors, and that is it can be executed in the evening under a strong light equally as well.

THE METHOD.

NE of the first steps in all branches of art work is to put in the values ; that is the darker shadows. Pay no attention to the high lights, they will take care of themselves. It may be well to state now the necessity of working at all times and upon all parts of the picture very lightly, as hard rubbing will produce a muddy effect. The lighter the touch the more transparent and beautiful the result.

Take one of the paper stomps, put it in the brass holder, rub it thoroughly in the crayon sauce, twisting it around until it is entirely covered with the sauce, on the point and tapering end : apply this first to the pupils of the eyes, the nostrils, and the line through the centre of the mouth. Next with a broad stroke (not a sharp one) to the lids of the eyes, the dark shades in the ears, and the eye-brows, following the outlines very carefully. The stomp having now cleaned itself somewhat is ready for the values in the face. In applying it to these shadows, do not use the point as you would a pencil, but rather broad strokes.

Tint the iris of the eyes, the shadows under the eyes, the curve in the nose and around the nostrils. Do this in little short strokes in one direction first, parallel to each other, afterwards crossing them at an acute angle, never at right angles. The shades in the cheeks and forehead are next in order, in the same manner. The work will appear rough and spotty at first, but these values are necessary. The cleaning up will be described later on. In shading the cheeks commence each stroke at the outline, working inwardly, and these may be curved slightly, hatching in the same manner at an acute angle boldly, yet so lightly that real lines are avoided. Look the face over thoroughly and put in all the darker shades, but not as strong as they will be required, as the work will look more transparent by gradually strengthening them, rather than in attempting to produce the proper strength at first.

Next put in the values of the hair, not in fine lines, but in broad strokes with the chamois stomp, but in this there should be no hatching. Make all the strokes in the direction in which the hair is combed. Leave the high lights as in the face, for the present. Watch the photograph closely, and put them on in the right place. In putting on any and all of these darker shades, either in hair, face, or drapery, always commence at the darkest part of such shadows and let the stomp move in the direction of the lighter. Now turn to the drapery. A black broadcloth coat, or a silk dress, should be worked in the same manner except it may be the latter can be finished a trifle finer. The drapery may be worked up with the chamois or paper stomp. The method of work is the same, as above described; short broad strokes crossing at an acute angle. Be careful not to make the strokes all one way.

In ending off the drapery, great care must be observed to have it grow lighter and lighter until it is lost entirely. It must not have the appearance of being cut off abruptly.

The background should be worked up in the same manner as the coat, only not so dark. Or it can be put in with the chamois pad, slightly tinted with the crayon sauce, and applied with a circular motion, commencing at the coat and face, and working away from them, gradually growing lighter and lighter, having no abrupt ending. Never make the background around the entire head in a bust picture, even if the subject has gray hair this is not necessary; it will have too much of a photographic appearance. Make the darkest background next to the highest light of the face. Artists differ very much in opinion upon the subject of backgrounds, and almost every one has a style of their own. Again nearly every portrait requires a different one, but generally all that is necessary is a light transparent atmosphere, varying in depth to suit the subject. A strong face well defined, and with dark hair and eyes, will bear a stronger background than one of a little child.

The drawing now, if the above directions have been followed carefully, has all the values, or principal shadows in their proper places. The next steps to be taken will improve its appearance.

THE DRAPERY.

THE drapery should receive its finishing touches first in order, leaving the face for the last. Take the chamois stomp, using the cleanest end, and borrowing color from the values, sweep it gently and lightly across the high-lights, in different directions, crossing them occasionally as previously described. Note the subject carefully and follow the modeling, to give the proper roundness, in the lappels of the coat, or folds in the dress. Having borrowed from the values, they may now need strengthening again. If the work thus far is very uneven, take the contè rubber with a fairly sharp point, and clean off the larger spots, using the rubber in the same manner as the stomp, hatching over these spots until the entire drapery is comparatively even, and of one general tone, darker toward the shoulders and neck, and ending very lightly if the subject be a vignette, otherwise of course cover the whole in imitation of the original. But bust portraits should always be vignetted. Details are not required in drapery, except perhaps the part nearest the face, as the collar, necktie, or other neck trimmings.

Neither attempt to imitate too closely the different styles of materials composing the same, except it may be in the forms of the folds, and the manner in which the light strikes them. By observing this rule it will not be difficult to decide of what material the drapery is composed.

To produce the effect desired the paper stomp should be used. Commence with considerable color, in the strongest shades first, hatching in short strokes, tolerably open, but not too much so. This produces a light and transparent appearance. It also gives depth, enables one to look into them, which would not be the effect if rubbed in too hard and closely. The entire drapery should be worked up in this manner, using the rubber to clean off the spots, filling up the lighter places with the stomp whenever required, and strengthening the extreme shadows, where they require it, by adding more color to the stomp. Do not leave the outlines of the shoulders too sharp, but go a little beyond them lightly to produce a soft and natural effect.

Study the original and you will notice generally a shade on the collar, and shirt-front; put these in evenly with the paper stomp. Lace work should not be followed with too much detail, but made somewhat indistinctly, with a piece of chamois slightly tinted, taking out the whiter spots or figures with the rubber, working for a general effect, as to the design of the figure, having it as a whole very delicate and soft. Many artists use white crayon in lace or embroidery work, but it is gradually going out of use. If a very strong white is required in any part of the drapery, or lace, and the rubber is not effectual in removing the crayon, take a very sharp knife and scrape the paper until the proper effect is produced.

If after following all these instructions the drapery does not appear quite as even or regular as may seem desirable, take the round contè crayon, and sharpen one end of it to a very fine point, place it in the brass holder, and go very lightly in little short strokes over the imperfect places, until the appearance is satisfactory.

Searles

PORTRAITS IN CRAYON.

STUDIO,

THE ART INSTITUTE,

200 MICHIGAN AVENUE,

CHICAGO,

⇒ THE ⇐

Smith · School · of · Music.

ROOM 2,

Central Music Hall, Chicago.

·o———— ❋ ————o·

C. JAY SMITH,

TEACHER OF SINGING,

(Late of the Royal Academy of Music, London.)

PIANO AND VIOLIN LESSONS BY COMPETENT TEACHERS

ALSO AN

Evening Class for reading Music at Sight.

MY ENGRAVED SCHOOL CARD

Is very handsome, containing a copy of one of Frank Bromley's last Paintings, with an Acrostic on the word Music, and will be sent free to any address on application.

J. B. CROCKER,

AUTHOR OF "CRAYON PORTRAITURE."

Artist in Crayon.

PORTRAIT WORK OF EVERY DESCRIPTION,

Including full and half length Pictures with Scenic Backgrounds, executed at reasonable rates.

CORRESPONDENCE BY MAIL SOLICITED.

Children's ✧ Pictures ✧ a ✧ Specialty

Instruction in Crayon Portraiture or Charcoal Drawing, given in classes, private lessons, or at pupil's residences, both day and evening.

Room 2, Central Music Hall,

CHICAGO.

The Metroscope.

From LOUIS MARXSEN, (now Mosher & Marxsen,) Chicago.

" Having used your squared glasses for enlarging, during the past year in my portrait work, I consider them the best possible means of rapidly obtaining a correct outline from a photograph or other small picture."

From A. F. BROOKS, Chicago.

" All photographs are more or less lengthened or broadened by the stretching of paper in mounting. The paper being made by machinery has a grain running lengthwise, and when dampened, like a shingle will widen. It is very noticable in some photographs, and usually in old ones the cards are lengthened and the cabinets are broadened, as the paper was cut to economise in printing. The only way this fault can be remedied in a drawing is by your system of squares, as the large squares can be elongated in either direction to hit the right proportion."

From ALFRED PAYNE, Chicago.

" I cheerfully commend the Metroscope devised by you to aid the Artist in working from the photograph. By its aid he can, with certainty, enlarge his model to any size, and make a correct copy by preserving all its relative proportions. While doing this, he is both exercising and dependent upon his 'eye,' and yet the combination of the squares of the Metroscope effectually prevent errors."

From C. F. SCHWERDT, Chicago.

" I made a trial of the Metroscope for the drawing of a portrait 60x72 inches of three children in a group, and found it a most valuable assistance, as I was enabled by it to get the drawing more correct than the photographs, as the paper had stretched the faces too wide."

From J. B. CROCKER, Author of "Crayon Portraiture."

" Although the principle of the Metroscope is by no means new, yet your improvements upon that principle are so radical as to virtually make it a new instrument, and really the most desirable one in the market for obtaining a correct enlargement."

From L. PRANG, (L. Prang & Co.) Boston.

" I heartily recommend the Metroscope for Lithographer's use in their Portrait work."

From FRED. BUEHRING, Editor "The Lithographer," Chicago.

" With the greatest pleasure we state that we know of no better medium for an Artist to obtain a correct drawing than by the means of your Metroscope."

From J. K. PUMPELLY, Chicago.

" It trains the eye, and should be used in all schools."

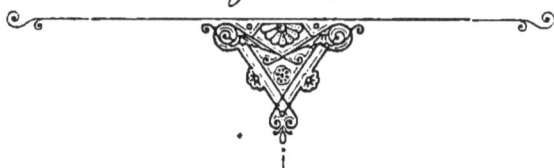

THURBER Art ⚜ Gallery

210 WABASH AVENUE, CHICAGO.

ART LOVERS

Are invited to call and examine my selection of Paintings, Engravings, Etchings, Etc., and if you want an Artistic Frame, I will be pleased to show our Styles.

E. L. STEVENSON & CO.

FINE ART MATERIALS.

OPPOSITE PALMER HOUSE.

69 MONROE STREET,

CHICAGO.

THAYER & CHANDLER,

IMPORTERS AND DEALERS IN

ARTISTS' MATERIALS,

DRAWING PAPERS, WAX FLOWER GOODS.

THE BÀCKGROUND.

HIS should next claim attention, and should be worked up in precisely the same manner or method, as described in the drapery, only not as dark, except the subject should have a white dress, then this rule should be reversed. This subject however is almost inexhaustible. The face is what should first attract the eye in a portrait, and anything which detracts from that, will injure the general effect, whether it be an elaborately finished collar, or pin, or a striking back-ground. Bear in mind that every other part of the picture is merely an accessory to the face, and therefore shall not have undue prominence.

If the picture be a Rembrandt it will bear a strong back-ground upon the side of the face where the light is strongest, while upon the darker side it should be lighter. Cloud rifts make a very pretty and effective back-ground for some subjects, but the outer and upper sides must always fade away with the utmost delicacy. A very sharp point may be used in cleaning up a back-ground if found necessary to give it an even tone. A few pictures will bear a solid black back-ground. This is made by first going over the entire surface of the paper or stretcher

3

around the picture, with a pad of chamois moderately blackened with the sauce, after which take the square conté crayon No. 3, place it on the broad flat surface of the side, and rub with a circular motion until the paper will hold no more. Then with the two fingers of the right hand go over it with the same circular motion until the surface is one unbroken mass of black. Be careful not to overrun the outlines and get spots on the face or drapery. Repeat this if necessary until the proper depth is produced.

Another method, if a greyish tint is desired, is to proceed as above with the black crayon, after which take a piece of soft white crayon, place it upon the stretcher in the same manner and proceed to rub this over the black, afterwards blending it with the fingers as before, and the result will be a grey, varying in shade in proportion to the predominance of the white or black. All such backgrounds however are easily injured, and should be framed and placed under the glass as soon as possible.

The subject of Scenic or Landscape backgrounds will be treated under its respective head.

THE HAIR.

N shading the hair only use the stomp in one direction, or back and forth if the crayon does not adhere to the paper well, and the effect will be seen at once. Endeavor to give the soft flow which hair should have. Avoid all lines, or any attempt to make individual hairs, as this would cause hard and wiry appearance, and destroy the softness and beauty of the picture.

Hair is best represented as it is in nature, in locks and masses. Borrow from the darker shades, and tint over the high lights with the chamois stomp, a little darker than necessary, and afterwards take out these high lights with the broad surface of the rubber. It may be found necessary to use the paper stomp before obtaining the proper finish, especially in working around the outside or outline of the head to complete its softness.

The color of the hair can only be represented by the different degrees of shade. White hair can be made exceedingly soft by using very little color, and doing most of the work with the rubber.

Mustache or whiskers are made in the same manner, in

masses, taking out the high lights with the rubber. Occassionally a few lines or single hairs may be put on with the point, both in the hair or the whiskers, when the picture is nearly finished, but all such must be put in very sparingly.

The drapery, background, and hair are supposed to be complete, excepting possibly a few finishing touches in the final softening effect.

THE EYES.

AKE the paper stomp slighly tinted with color, and proceed to finish the eyes. Bear in mind, the method of applying this to all parts of the features should be in short strokes, very lightly crossing them at an acute angle, using care not to have them too oblique, and never at right angles. Begin with the upper lids, darken them slightly, and working upward and away from them toward the eyebrows. Strengthen the pupil all that is possible, and proceed to tint the iris, making the upper part of it darker in shade than the lower, as there is always a shadow cast upon it by the eyelid. The lower lid should not consist of a line, it is formed by the shading above and below it. Study very carefully the original picture, and note all the peculiarities of form and expression. Leave the catch lights in their proper places if possible. This, however, is optional, as they can easily be made after they eyes are finished by scratching them with a knife; or they can be put in with Chinese White on the tip of a brush. Darken the corners, and tint very lightly the ball, this should never be left perfectly white. If during the work, any part becomes too dark, or spots are left, lighten such, and take off the spots with the rubber.

The eyebrows should be put on in the same manner as the hair, but be careful to tone them down to the proper depth gradually, and preserve the form or shape. Next take a clean paper or chamois stomp, and pass it smoothly and broadly back and forth over the lids of the eyebrows, going a little beyond the latter on the forehead. This tends to give softness, and blends these shadows off into or toward the high lights, thus giving the roundness desired. In the iris, there should be opposite the catch light, a lighter tone called reflected light; the remainder of the iris should be shaded to a greater or less degree, according to the subject. The pupil can now be strengthened by using the contè crayon point, making it a very deep black.

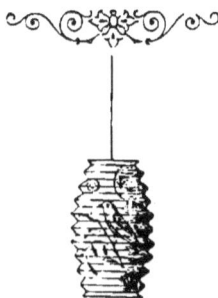

THE NOSE.

THERE should always be a dark shadow under the eyebrows toward the nose; borrow from this to shade the sides; put in the nostrils, using care to have them the proper shape, but not quite so large as the outline, as the remainder will work into a half tone when blending, and give the proper roundness. Work away from them now and give the curves to the lower part of the nose, and blend the nostrils until the proper shape is produced. Carry up the tones toward the eyes and off slightly toward the cheeks.

Remember if a wrong movement is made, or too much color put on, the rubber will soon restore it to its proper tint. Leave the easel occasionally and view the work from a little distance.

In all well lighted photographs, one side of the face is in stronger shadow than the other, this must be noticed in shading the nose, and if carefully executed and well modeled the nose will appear to stand out from the face in a natural manner.

THE MOUTH.

THIS is one of the important features of the face, and great care should be exercised not to lose the expression in working it up.

Firmness and strength in the masculine and sweetness and delicacy in the feminine. Do not make a hard line through the lips, but begin at the corners, make those the strongest, working from them with a lighter touch to the centre, where the greatest fullness lies, and at this central point there is generally a slight curve, which must be carefully preserved. Make the shadows, half tints, and lights, in exact imitation of the original. Avoid all hard outlines in the lips, by working up to the outlines very carefully; in fact there is not a single line in the whole face. Seeming lines or bounderies are caused by the sharp approach of light and shade.

THE FOREHEAD.

T HE process of putting in the shadows in the forehead, is precisely the same as has already been described ; short strokes, slightly curved at the temples ; clearing off the spots, and filling up the large lighter spots, until the work looks clean and yet moderately open. Soften the hair where it falls upon the forehead, or where it joins the face about the temples. Do not be afraid of losing the line of where the hair commences, or the forehead begins. It wants to be lost. It must be soft to make the picture artistic and natural. Generally the strongest light in any picture is on the forehead.

If the subject should be that of an elderly face, many wrinkles will be noticed. These are put on boldly at first with the paper stomp in their exact position, after which soften them above and below, with a clean stomp, and if too strong lighten them with a finely pointed rubber.

THE FACE.

THE blending of the values in the face should now receive attention. The deepest shades should not be carried to the extreme outline of the face. There is always a reflected light which will escape the notice of the beginner, if strict attention is not given.

This is often the case in the forehead and the chin as well as the cheeks.

Remember there must be no distinct or abrupt ending of any shadow, each one must blend off gradually into the other, or in the high light. As a general rule the high lights should not be left with the pure white shade of the paper. They should all be tinted, although so lightly it will be almost impossible to decide whether they have received any tint at all. There are many half tones however which must be preserved. No special instructions are required in regard to the ears, the work should be the same as described for the other features ; preserve the form and shape of the shadows, and blend to give softness and roundness.

FINISHING.

THE final finishing touches can now be given. Look the work over carefully, and soften all the outlines or outer edges of every part of the picture. Do this with the small paper stomp, fairly clean. Examine all the deeper shades, and strengthen all that may seem to require it, or lighten such as may be too dark.

The stomp and rubber will alone be required for this work. It would be well to rub the paper stomp on the block of sand paper to soften it slightly. The rubber should also be trimmed with a knife, after which rub off the sharp edges on the sand paper, and have it moderately sharp at the point. If any white spots are noticeable in any of the shadows, either in the face, drapery, or background, fill those up to the desired tone with the stomp. If any of the hatching appears too broad or too open, fill that up slightly. Take out any desired high lights in the hair with the rubber, as such are much more effective than they would be if any attempt was made to leave them during the progress of working.

Any outline that appears too hard or cutting, soften it

by working upon the edges a little beyond, for every part must be round and soft. There must also be strength as well as softness; and color of the eyes or hair, can alone be represented by light and shade.

It is these finishing touches which will, in a great measure, give to the portrait its life and beauty. Study your picture from a distance, and note when a few touches will improve its appearance. Examine the drapery, the high lights on the collar, or the lace, clear up any places that may have become rubbed, and leave no spots or specks to mar the clear and even effect of the work. These little touches may seem insignificant, but they will greatly enhance its value.

In conclusion, remember that skill can only be acquired by continued practice. Be willing to spoil several pictures if necessary, to acquire the art at last. Consider it a necessity to learn to draw. In " Hunt's Talks on Art," he says : " Any one who can make the letter D, can learn to draw. Learning to draw is learning the grammar of a language." Study the faces upon the street, note the shadows and high lights, and thus become familiar with the human features. Read these instructions over carefully and studiously, and follow them step by step, for no amount of labor is too great to accomplish the object desired.

It might be well to advise the student to make several

outlines of the same subject. In the first one put in the values, making them comparatively clean, and blending the edges off upon the high lights. Leave it in this unfinished state.

In the second, put in the same values, strengthening and modeling them, to give the roundness and form. The third and fourth should be carried each one a little farther toward completion, and the last one may be finished in all its details. Hang these up side by side in the order in which they come, and they will be found of great practical value, as a key from which to obtain such knowledge as may be desired; while the practice itself will enable you to use the stomps with greater freedom.

POINT WORK.

MANY artists do not use the point in finishing a crayon portrait, and even such as do employ it, nearly all have a method peculiarly their own. In all cases however it should be done with a long finely pointed crayon, very lightly.

It is often used in a gliding motion in different directions, so lightly and so openly that the grain of the paper only catches the crayon, but great care must be taken to preserve the evenness of the tone, leaving no spots that are darker than the others. Again a very fine effect is produced by lightly hatching the face, after the manner of using the stomp, curving the strokes in the direction of the fibers of the flesh ; namely, horizontal on the forehead, perpendicular on the nose, and circular around the eyes, mouth and general contour of the face. All such strokes should begin lightly, and end lightly, and should be regular and parallel to each other, crossing at acute angles. But all point work requires a vast amount of practice, and it would be best for the student to become proficient in stomp work, before attempting the use of the point. By proper use of the paper stomp and rubber, an effect can be produced almost if not quite equal to the point.

FULL LENGTH PORTRAITS.

FULL length portraiture is a different branch of work, and requires more study. Yet it is generally the desire of every artist who acquires skill in portrait work, to be able to execute a full or half length figure.

The first requirement will be to draw the enlargement. A Solar Print may be obtained and used to trace the outline, but these are quite expensive. The system of squares described in this work is an excellent one. The outlines having been obtained, transfer it to the stretcher according to the directions heretofore given, and preserve them with the paper stomp. A large, soft rolled, chamois stomp will be the most convenient for the drapery and background, in putting in the values, but in finishing and blending, the paper stomp may again be employed.

The chamois rolled up in a little pad is often used in putting in these values, as greater rapidity is the result. Care should be exercised however not to rub too hard, or the effect would be muddy, and also use it with a circular motion. White dresses are generally worked up entirely

with a small piece of chamois, and the broad surface of
the rubber, to take out the high lights.   Avoid details in
lace work, and do not use white crayon, the white paper is
the most effective.

The same rules may be applied to head dresses, bonnets,
feathers, or flowers.   These are all worked up in the same
manner, and the rubber is one of the most important
factors for the high lights.

Heavy robes of velvet should first be made with the
chamois pad, after which apply the stick of No. 3 crayon,
putting it on in a solid mass, and then blending it with
the fingers.   In such kind of drapery, the white crayon
may be applied to the high lights in the same manner as
the black, and using the finger to blend it with the black,
to form the half tones in modeling, after the manner of
Pastel work.   In full length portraits more of the details
are worked up, such as necklaces, chains, or ornaments on
the dress, and the paper stomp will here be found the
most useful.

SCENIC BACKGROUNDS.

FULL length portraits require as a general rule a scenic background. Yet care must be exercised that the figure must be the principal object, and not the background. It should be quiet and unobtrusive, receding far behind the head of the portrait. Any objects that may be introduced should be shadowy and indistinct. If a landscape background is desired, the trees and shrubbery should be light and indistinct, excepting in the immediate foreground, where a little greater attention may be given to the details. Interiors are sometimes introduced with pieces of furniture or drapery. Such may be worked up much darker, after the manner described in the drapery of the figure, with the crayon stick and fingers.

Stone columns are worked with the paper stomp and rubber, giving it the appearance of rough stone, by putting on the color in little rough dashes or spots, and taking out the high lights with the rubber in the same manner.

4

There is no end to the variety of scenic backgrounds, and it would be impossible to describe the scenes or objects that may be introduced which might be in harmony with the subject.   Such must be left to the taste and skill of the artist.   They may go through all the possible gradations from a shadow on a wall, to the depth and obscurity surrounding a figure standing in an open door or window.

The only instructions to be given may be summed up in these words; preserve the same delicacy and softness that is described in working up the figure; avoid all hard lines or abrupt endings, and have the entire background subservient to the figure.

TO FIX CRAYON DRAWINGS.

VERY much has already been written upon this subject, and there is great danger in any and all the methods. The safer plan is to leave the work in its simple state, and protect it by a frame and glass. Many of the methods of fixing result in a flattening of the tones and high lights, thus destroying its brilliancy and depth, often making it necessary to retouch many parts of the picture to give it additional force. But if found desirable in order to preserve a number of drawings, the "Fixative," for sale at the Art Stores will be found the most convenient.

GENERAL REMARKS.

MASTER the foregoing instructions in their entirety, and follow them carefully. The practice thus derived will train the hand to follow the dictation of the eye.

To write or copy any written language the hand must first be taught to follow the forms of each letter, and the same may be said to be true in drawing; the practice will enable the hand to make the necessary strokes without any hesitation or uncertainty. The object of this treatise has been to give practical instruction, in as simple a manner as possible, and it now remains for the student to make the best use of the information given.

Practice and perseverance will enable any one of average intelligence, combined with a love for the art, to obtain excellence in executing natural and life-like portraits.

LANDSCAPE DRAWING.

IT is presumed that many who read the foregoing pages, and put into practice the instruction given, will naturally feel inclined to take an occasional excursion for pleasure, and sail away from the imitative art, or the simple copying from drawings and photographs, and look around for natural objects to reproduce upon the sketch book. The principles of landscape or object drawing are the same as described for the human face. It must have first the outline, and then light and shade ; the outline gives the form and shape, while the light and shade give the roundness and strength. Sketch the outline boldly, yet as accurately as possible, with a lead pencil, or better still with a piece of charcoal. Do not take hold near the point, but at the farther end, very loosely, to give perfect freedom to the arm and hand. Charcoal can be very easily removed from the paper by using a soft piece of flannel, therefore make all corrections necessary ; when complete, save them by going over them lightly with the paper stomp. Next put in the masses or values. This can be done with the charcoal if desired, and strengthened with the stomp in the same manner described in putting in the values in the human face. Leave all details for the finishing. For sky or clouds, use the chamois pad, or a soft chamois stomp; the flat tints of trees or mountains the same.

After putting in all the values, the detail work may commence. Use the small paper stomps for all such, but very little detail must be put into a landscape, except the immediate foreground. All outlines must be soft and indistinct. The foliage of trees can be made very effective with the stomp and rubber. The point can be used if desired in cleaning up the spotty places, or the whole picture worked over with the point, in short, regular, blunt, but soft lines, thus giving the inclinations of mountain slopes, or rugged rocks. But a much softer effect will be produced with the stomp, excepting in very deep or rich shadows; then use the point, and cross hatch to give the necessary strength. But after all the rules or instructions laid down in this book were formed from practice, and although the student may feel content to receive this instruction from another, yet the best method, and the most valuable instruction, is PRACTICE.

CHARCOAL DRAWING.

THE use of charcoal for landscape or figure drawing is becoming more and more popular every year. Its use is easy to learn, and the results are very satisfactory. It is one of the modern arts; the old masters employed it for sketching principally, although there are in existence a few examples in simple charcoal.

The paper is of a different quality or grain from that used on crayon work. It should be of a yellow white tint, and a fine and even grain. If too rough the charcoal will catch too strongly, while on the other hand if it is too smooth, it will not produce a good shading. Like paper for crayon work, it should be stretched. The materials necessary are the small paper stomps, a chamois stomp, linen and woolen rags, bread crumbs, and the rubber. The sticks of charcoal considered the best are the French, either the Contè or Rouget. There are two methods, the first when the stomp is used throughout the entire drawing; the other by using the sticks sharply pointed, and cross hatching, discarding the stomp entirely.

The former is the most popular, and will make the softer picture. Take one of the larger sticks, cut the end flat and broad, and commencing on the top of the stretcher, make an even and regular tone over the whole surface of the paper. Now take the first three fingers of the right hand, and commencing at the bottom, spread the charcoal over the paper, going from right to left, until the whole is one flat tone, resembling a wash of india ink.

If this leaves the tone too dark, go over it with the clean linen rag, softly; this operation of putting on the charcoal and using the fingers or rag, may be repeated until the desired depth of tone is produced.

The next step is to put in the deeper tones or masses with the charcoal stick, and rubbing it down with the stomp. This process may often have to be repeated several times to get sufficient depth. The high lights are obtained by using the woolen rag for the half tones, and the rubber or bread crumbs for the stronger lights. Work up details afterward with a piece of finely pointed charcoal.

Although the tones of charcoal are more opaque than crayon, yet they possess a velvety richness and softness which crayon will not give, and for landscape drawing it is especially valuable. It has other advantages over oil or water colors; being dry it necessitates no delays, and therefore a landscape can be drawn with wonderful rapidity.

Any part that is unsatisfactory can be easily effaced ; in fact the drawing may be a succession of alterations, changes, modifications of tone or shade, until it meets approval. It is often used in portrait work, and especially is it adapted for the portraits of children, where delicacy and softness are essential.

The entire process of working in charcoal is so simple that scarcely any instructions are necessary. All charcoal drawings must be fixed, and if care is used the most con- venient method is direct fixation. This Fixatif can be obtained at the Art Stores, and is used by blowing a fine spray over the drawing, as perfumes are diffused through an atomizer. It may be necessary to repeat the operation several times, waiting each time for the paper to dry. Charcoal drawing, it should be remembered, must only render effects, not details.

The amateur will find this the most difficult lesson to learn. To illustrate this point we quote the following from a celebrated teacher. " You see a beautiful sunset, and a barn comes into your picture. Will you grasp the whole at once, in a grand sweep of broad sky, and a broad mass of dark building, or will you stop to draw in all the shingles on the barn, perhaps even the nails on each shingle ; pos- sibly the shady side of each nail? Your fine sunset is all gone while you are doing this." Forget the little things in a picture, and try to see only the grand broad masses, and put off all details until the last; and if it should happen that every feather on a bird was not in exact position, or one leaf lacking on a tree, it will not be noticed. With a paper stomp, a piece of charcoal, and a piece of rubber, a picture can be made, and a beautiful one too, without a line or scarcely a bit of detail in it.

In closing this treatise it may be well to say, do not become discouraged after the first few efforts; if the desire to learn to draw is strong, rest assured success will come by patient practice. Do not confine yourself to the instructions contained in this work. Do not be afraid to try experiments, and see what the effects may be. In this way one's own individuality will show in the results, and such results will be valuable because they are original.

CONCLUSION.

IT may hardly seem necessary to add to this treatise anything more in the way of instruction. Doubtless many who read these pages will undertake the study of Portraiture as an amusement or recreation simply. But the author would advise the student to make it a serious study, and not rest content after being able to execute a moderately fair portrait. Every year shows an increasing interest in all Art matters, and Portraiture should be considered in the light of an accomplishment. The fact that others are far ahead, should only act as an incentive for greater labor and study.

The student should bear in mind there are two distinct lessons to be learned in following the instructions here given ; first the method of work, or the manner of putting the crayon upon the paper ; second, to preserve the exact likeness of the original. Therefore study the subject thoroughly and carefully ; this is very essential in obtaining a correct and pleasing likeness. If this has been attended to in the early stages of the work the likeness will not be difficult of attainment. The object and ·aim of this treatise has been to present the instruction in the simplest manner possible, knowing full well that the smallest details often prove the most valuable to the student.

◄◦Artistic Printing.◦►

_____

THE JEWELERS' JOURNAL,

57 Washington Street,

CHICAGO.

www.ingramcontent.com/pod-product-compliance
Lightning Source LLC
Chambersburg PA
CBHW022142090426
42742CB00010B/1352